W9-BAI-726

ABIGAIL

This book belongs to:

Abby Camille

Nursery Rhymes

Precious Moments®

rhymes adapted
& illustrated by
Sam Butcher

Baker Books

A Division of Baker Book House Co
Grand Rapids, Michigan 49516

Art © 1979, 1981, 1987, 1996 by Precious Moments, Inc.
Text © 1999 by Baker Book House

Published by Baker Books
a division of Baker Book House Company
P.O. Box 6287, Grand Rapids, MI 49516-6287

Printed in the United States of America

All rights reserved. No part of this publication may be reproduced, stored in a retrieval system, or transmitted in any form or by any means—for example, electronic, photocopy, recording—without the prior written permission of the publisher. The only exception is brief quotations in printed reviews.

Library of Congress Cataloging-in-Publication Data

Precious Moments nursery rhymes / illustrated by Sam Butcher.
    p.   cm.
    Contents: Old Mother Hubbard—Twinkle, twinkle little star—Rain, rain, go away—Rub a dub, dub—Jack, be nimble—Mary, Mary—Little Bo Peep—Hush-a-bye baby—There was an old lady.
    ISBN 0-8010-4426-X
    1. Nursery rhymes. 2. Children's poetry. [1. Nursery rhymes.] I. Butcher, Samuel J. (Samuel John), 1939–   ill.
PZ8.3.P88935   1999
398.8—dc21   98-54775

For current information about all releases from Baker Book House, visit our web site:
                    http://www.bakerbooks.com

EMPTY

# Rhymes to Read

other Goose's rhymes have been passed down from great-grandparent to grandparent to parent to child for many years. Children all around the world have heard her stories.

Mother Goose's stories are part of your life too: on the playground outside or inside on rainy days, in the morning while you play or at night before you go to sleep. These rhymes are part of your days and nights, and the characters have become your friends.

A poor mother and her pretty puppy. A bright star that stands out in the sky. Merry raindrops we send away today but invite back tomorrow. A jolly old king with lots of friends and riches. Three men sailing the ocean in a most unusual boat. A small boy who jumps very high. A special girl with a special garden.

A young shepherd girl whose sheep
adore her. A little baby gently rocking
    to sleep. An old woman who lives
    in a shoe.

        Come and see these friends again.
You've heard their stories many times before.
But they take a different twist in this book as
we look in a new way at how God cares for
them all. Remember as you read that God
cares for you too!

Old Mother Hubbard
Went to the cupboard
To get her poor puppy a bone.
So she said a short prayer
Before she got there,
And praise the Lord,
There was one.

moon

winkle, twinkle,
little star,
Oh, how lovely
   that you are.
God created
   you to shine
Like a diamond
   for all time.

ain, rain,
go away.
But if you come
another day,
Touch every flower
with your love
With raindrops falling
from above.

Old King Cole
was a merry old soul.
A merry old soul was he,
Because he was blessed
with good friends
and success
In a kingdom
of pure harmony.

Rub a dub, dub,
three men in a tub
Sailed away
on the ocean blue.
But they were not afraid
because they all made
A great team
and a wonderful crew.

ack be nimble,

Jack be quick.

Jack jumped over

the candlestick,

Because to jump

and exercise

Will make you healthy,

strong, and wise.

ary, Mary,

so extraordinary,

How does your

garden grow?

With plenty of love,

and rain from above.

That's how my dear

garden grows.

Little Bo Peep
takes care of her sheep
And always knows where
to find them.
Her sheep never roam
too far from their home
Because Bo Peep is always
behind them.

Hush-a-bye baby
in the treetop,
When the wind blows,
the cradle will rock.
When the bough swings
so gently and sweet,
Baby will safely and
tenderly sleep.

There was an old lady
who lived in a shoe.
She had so many children
    she didn't know what to do.
So she asked God to help her
    and show his great love
By blessing her house
    with his help from above.

Now after these stories
it's finally time
for you to start
drifting away
On the wings of your dreams
and to nod off to sleep
Till tomorrow—
a brand-new day!